The Phoenicians: The History and Culture of One of the Ancient World's Most Influential Civilizations

By Charles River Editors

A Phoenician sarcophagus dated back to the 5th century BC

About Charles River Editors

Charles River Editors provides superior editing and original writing services across the digital publishing industry, with the expertise to create digital content for publishers across a vast range of subject matter. In addition to providing original digital content for third party publishers, we also republish civilization's greatest literary works, bringing them to new generations of readers via ebooks.

Sign up here to receive updates about free books as we publish them, and visit Our Kindle Author Page to browse today's free promotions and our most recently published Kindle titles.

Introduction

An ancient amphora depicting the tale of Cadmus

The Phoenicians

"These people, who had formerly dwelt on the shores of the Erythraean Sea, having migrated to the Mediterranean and settled in the parts which they now inhabit, began at once, they say, to adventure on long voyages, freighting their vessels with the wares of Egypt and Assyria..." - Herodotus

Of all the peoples of the ancient Near East, the Phoenicians are among the most recognizable but also perhaps the least understood. The Phoenicians never built an empire like the Egyptians and Assyrians; in fact, the Phoenicians never created a unified Phoenician state but instead existed as independent city-state kingdoms scattered throughout the Mediterranean region. However, despite the fact there was never a "Phoenician Empire," the Phoenicians proved to be more prolific in their exploration and colonization than any other peoples in world history until the Spanish during the Age of Discovery.

The Phoenicians were well-known across different civilizations throughout the ancient world, and their influence can be felt across much of the West today because they are credited with inventing the forerunner to the Greek alphabet, from which the Latin alphabet was directly derived. Nonetheless, the Phoenicians left behind few written texts, so modern historians have been forced to reconstruct their past through a variety of ancient Egyptians, Assyrian, Babylonian, Greek, and Roman sources. It's not even clear what the Phoenicians called themselves, because the name "Phoenician" is derived from the Greek word "phoinix", which possibly relates to the dyes they produced and traded (Markoe 2000, 10). The mystery of the ancient Phoenicians is further compounded by the fact that archaeologists have only been able to excavate small sections of the three primary Phoenician cities: Byblos, Sidon, and Tyre.

Despite the inherent problems in reconstructing Phoenician history, there are enough primary sources available to accurately place the Phoenician people in their proper historical context within the ancient Near East, and scholars have found that given their extensive exploration, colonization, trade, and manufacturing (among other things), the Phoenicians deserve to be considered alongside the other well-known peoples of antiquity.

The Phoenicians: The History and Culture of One of the Ancient World's Most Influential Civilizations comprehensively covers the history, culture, and lingering mysteries behind the Phoenicians, profiling their origins and their lasting legacy.. Along with pictures of important people, places, and events, you will learn about the Phoenicians like never before, in no time at all.

The Phoenicians: The History and Culture of One of the Ancient World's Most Influential Civilizations

About Charles River Editors

Introduction

Chapter 1: The Origins of the Phoenicians

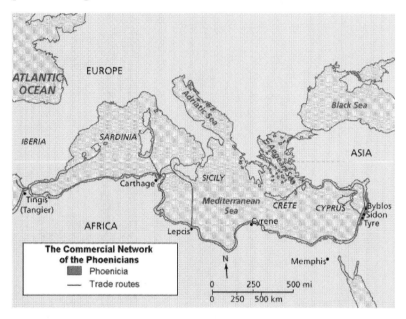

Map of Phoenicia and Phoenician trade routes

Since the Phoenicians never developed a historiographical tradition like that of the Egyptians and Mesopotamians, determining their origins is problematic at best and can only be approached through a combination of philology, historiography, and archaeology. Of course, it must also be remembered that when scholars analyze the historical texts of other peoples who wrote about the Phoenicians, they have to keep in mind that foreign writers likely had biases about the people they were describing.

Nowhere is this concept more apparent than in the Bible, thanks to two verses from the Old Testament that cast the Phoenicians in a negative light: "And Ahab the son of Omri did evil in the sight of the Lord above all that were before him. And it came to pass, as if it had been a light thing for him to walk in the sins of Jeroboam the son of Nebat, that he took to wife Jezebel the daughter of Ethba'al king of the Sidonians, and went and served Ba'al, and worshipped him" (1 Kings 16: 30-31). Unfortunately, these two verses have been used throughout history to depict the Phoenicians as licentious heathens, when the reality is that many other Biblical verses depict the Phoenicians as being quite adept in the arts of ancient statecraft and oftentimes allies of the Israelites (as will be discussed further below).

Another ancient historical source that is questionable in its accuracy of Phoenician origins (but not as biased) comes from the 5th century BC Greek historian Herodotus. In his seminal *Histories*, Herodotus wrote, "These people came originally from the so-called Red Sea: and as soon as they had penetrated to the Mediterranean and settled in the country where they are today, they took to making long trading voyages. Loaded with Egyptian and Assyrian goods, they called at various places along the coast including Argos, in those days the most important place in the land now called Hellas" (Herodotus, *Histories,* I, 1). Although most scholars discount the Red Sea origins of the Phoenicians, who occupied the Levantine coast of the Mediterranean Sea during ancient times, Herodotus' account of Phoenician trade and colonization can be corroborated by multiple primary sources.

Today, scholars believe that the origins of the Phoenician people can be traced closer to their homeland of Phoenicia, and they have generally used the ancient Phoenician language as a way to determine the ancient civilization's origins. The ancient Phoenician language was Semitic and very closely related to Hebrew and Aramaic, which were the other two major ancient Semitic languages of the Levant (Moscati 1968, 91), and due to the linguistic similarities, scholars believe that the Phoenicians shared a common ancestry with the Hebrews and they were both known as Canaanites before they became Phoenicians and Israelites (Markoe 2000, 10).

Although philology has allowed the linguistic origins of the Phoenicians to be unlocked, their geographic origins will continue to be debated until more conclusive archeological evidence is discovered, which might hopefully happen in the near future since the modern discovery of ancient Phoenicia is still relatively new. The modern discovery and study of the ancient Phoenicians did not begin in earnest until 1860, when Emperor Napoleon III of France led a punitive military expedition into Lebanon against members of the Islamic Druze sect, which had just massacred members of the Maronite Christian sect (Herm 1975, 27). Perhaps inspired by his grandfather, Napoleon Bonaparte, who led both French troops and scholars into Egypt in 1799, Napoleon III brought his own scholars, namely Ernest Renan, to study the ancient ruins of the cities of coastal Lebanon (Herm 1975, 27).

Portrait of Napoleon III

Ernest Renan

Unlike Egypt, which has a number of intact ancient monuments for scholars to study (especially in Upper Egypt), the major ancient Phoenician cities had been thoroughly built over in medieval and modern times, but this problem did not deter Renan, and his efforts later drew other renowned historians and archaeologists to Lebanon. After World War I, when Lebanon was briefly ruled by the French under a League of Nations mandate, more scholars traveled there in order to try to unlock the mysteries of Phoenicia, and the most famous early 20th century scholar to study the ancient Phoenician ruins was the esteemed French Egyptologist Pierre Montet, who used his knowledge of ancient history and modern archeological techniques to uncover some monuments from Byblos (Herm 1975, 29).

Pierre Montet

Although World War II and modern development hampered extensive archaeological expeditions of the major Phoenician cities, Renan and Montet's early efforts helped to open Phoenician history to the modern world. It was soon revealed that the three Phoenician cities of Byblos, Tyre, and Sidon were the backbone of ancient Phoenician culture.

Chapter 2: The Major Cities of Ancient Phoenicia

Most of the ancient Phoenician cities were located along the coastline of what are today the modern nation nations of Israel and Lebanon, with Byblos being the farthest to the north, Tyre at the south end, and Sidon between the two. Early in Phoenician history, Byblos was the most important of the three cities, and the oldest known historical mention of the city is on the ancient Egyptian "Palermo Stone," which is dated to the reign of the Fourth Dynasty Egyptian king Snefru (ca. 2613 BC) (Herm 1975, 34). Since quality wood was rare in Egypt, the Egyptians coveted the timber, especially cedar, from the mountains of Phoenicia to use for building their large river boats, furniture, and temple architecture. In exchange, the Egyptians traded gold, which was plentiful in Egypt, for the valuable wood (Lucas and Harris 1999, 432-34). The reciprocal trade relationship continued for centuries, but it changed drastically when the Egyptian king Thutmose III (ca. 1490-1436) came to the throne.

G. Dallorto's picture of the Palermo Stone

Thutmose III was the fourth king of Egypt's Eighteenth Dynasty during the New Kingdom, and his reign ushered in a period of imperial greatness for Egypt. It was also a time when the great powers of the ancient Near East, such as Egypt, the Hittites, and Babylon, divided up the smaller kingdoms in the region amongst themselves (Kuhrt 2010, 1:283-331). Unfortunately for Byblos, and most of Phoenicia, they were among the smaller kingdoms that fell under Egyptian control. Thutmose III led several campaigns personally into Retenu, which was one of the Egyptian words for Phoenicia, in order to quell rebellions, facilitate trade, and exact tribute, and the historical records show that there was no question what the master and subordinate positions were in the Egyptian-Phoenician relationship. The historical annals of Thutmose III from the Karnak Temple detail the submission of Phoenician princes during his seventh campaign: "Tribute of the princes of Retenu, who came to do obeisance to the [souls] of his majesty in this year: - slaves, male and female; . . . of this country; silver , 761 deben, 2 kidet; 19 chariots, wrought with silver; the equipment of their weapons of war; 104 oxen with bullocks; 172 calves and cows; total, 276; 4,622 small cattle; native copper, 40 blocks; lead, . . . 41 golden bracelets, figured with . . .; together with all their produce and all the fine fragrant woods of this country" (Breasted 2001, 199).

This text, and others from the annals of Thutmose III, clearly show the inferior political status that the Phoenicians had vis-à-vis the Egyptians during the New Kingdom from an Egyptian perspective, but a collection of texts known as the "Amarna Letters" also depicts the relationship from the perspective of the king of Byblos. The Amarna Letters are a number of diplomatic documents that were written on clay tablets in the cuneiform script of the Akkadian language during the mid-to-late second millennium BC (Cochavi-Rainey 1999, 1), and the tablets are named the Amarna Letters because they were discovered in the ruins of the Egyptian city of Amarna in 1887 (Cochavi-Rainey 1999, 1). The tone of the letters between the great powers such as Egypt and Babylon is that of equity, but those between a great power and a lesser power, such as Egypt and the Phoenician cities, clearly demonstrates a hierarchy of power.

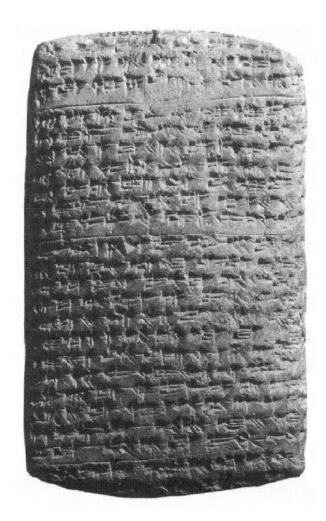

Picture of one of the Amarna Letters

In one letter, the king of Gubla (the ancient Egyptian word for Byblos) requests military support from the Egyptian king in order to deal with a marauding tribe called the Apiru. The letter states: [Ri]b Hadda says to his lord, king of all countries, Great King: May the Lady of Gubla grant power to my lord. I fall at the feet of my lord, my Sun, 7 times and 7 times. May the king, my lord, know that Gubla (ie: Byblos), the maidservant of the king from ancient times, is safe and sound. The war, however, of the Apiru against me is severe. (Our) sons and daughters and the furnishings of the houses are gone, since they have been sold [in] the land of Yarimuta for our provisions to keep us alive. 'For the lack of a cultivator, my field is like a woman without a husband.' I have written repeatedly to the palace because of the illness afflicting me, [but there is no one] who has looked at the words that keep arriving. May the king give heed [to] the words of [his] servant... ...The Apiru killed Ad[una the king] of Irqata-(Arqa), but there was no one who said anything to Abdi-Ashirta, and so they go on taking (territory for themselves). Miya, the ruler of Arašni, seized Ar[d]ata, and just now the men of Ammiy have killed their lord. I am afraid. May the king be informed that the king of Hatti has seized all the countries that were vassals of the king of Mitan...Send arc[hers]" (Moran 1992, 137-38).

Even more than 3,000 years later, readers cringe at the extreme obeisance that the king of Byblos demonstrates in the letter towards the king of Egypt, who as other letters reveals, was not too quick to come to the Phoenician city's aide. The follow up letter reads, "Rib-Hadda says to [his] lord, king of all countries, Great King, King of Battle . . . The king, however, has now withdrawn his support of his loyal city. May the king inspect the tablets of his father's house (for the time) when the ruler in Gubla was not a loyal servant. Do not be negligent of your servant. Behold, the war of the Apiru against (me) is severe and, as the gods of y[our] land [are ali]ve, our sons and daughters (as well as we ourselves) are gone since they have been sold in the land of Yarimuta for provisions to keep us alive" (Moran, 1992, 142-43).

One of Rib-Hadda's letters to the Egyptian pharaoh Akhenaten

The Amarna Letters and the annals of Thutmose III demonstrate that Byblos was dependent and subservient to Egypt for hundreds of years, but the texts do not indicate the fact that the Phoenician city remained a wealthy city during this period as well. Archaeological evidence shows that during the period of Egyptian domination, ancient Byblos was a walled city that had both a land and a sea gateway (Herm 1975, 31). The city planning was quite advanced for the time, as the streets ran concentrically to the town center and canals carried rain and drainage water away. The limited modern excavations of the city have also revealed a number of exquisite funerary offerings that indicate the inhabitants of Byblos, although subordinate to Egypt, prospered financially and materially from the relationship (Herm 1975, 31).

A Bronze Age jug found in Byblos from the period

When Egypt lost its imperial possessions at the end of the New Kingdom (ca. 1075 BC), Byblos was lost with it, and in many ways the Phoenician city declined in importance as Tyre then became the most important city in Phoenicia. From ca. 1200-1000 BC, the eastern Mediterranean region was devastated by a series of migrations and raids by a group of disparate peoples known collectively as the Sea Peoples (Morkot 1996, 30-31). The Sea Peoples managed to inflict heavy damage on the Egyptians, Hittites, and Mycenaeans, but for reasons unknown to modern scholars, the area of Phoenicia was hardly affected despite being located in the middle of the invasion zone (Stern 1990, 30). In fact, it appears that the Sea Peoples' raids may have inadvertently helped the Phoenicians, who were subsequently able to take over the trade of destroyed neighboring cities such as Ugarit (Bikai 1989, 204).

It was immediately after this period, which coincided with the beginning of the Iron Age, that Tyre became an international power under King Hiram I (971-939 BC). Under Hiram I, Tyre eclipsed the power and influence of Byblos and Sidon partially due to the relations the king fostered with the ancient kingdom of Israel; Hiram I traded extensively with Israel under the reigns of Solomon and David, and the timber used to build the Solomonic Temple was supplied by Hiram (as discussed more thoroughly below) (Markoe 2000, 33).

Perhaps the greatest achievement of Hiram I's reign was the transfer of the entire city of Tyre from the shore to the sea (Herm 1975, 65). Since the city was built on a man-made island, the project must have required thousands of men and taken many years to handle all of the filling material needed to be brought from the mainland (Herm 1975, 66). Other factors also had to be considered, including the problem of drinking water. The Tyrians solved the problem a number of ways, including bringing drinking water from the mainland, using rain-catching cisterns, and capturing fresh water from the sea bed by using funnels and leather pipes (Herm 1975, 68). Incredibly, the thriving city was built on an area that is estimated to be no bigger than 40 acres (Bikai 1989, 206).

Hiram I rebuilt Tyre into a phenomenal and powerful city, but of almost equal importance in the land of Phoenicia was Sidon, which was also dependent on the sea for its livelihood. Sidon was built on a flat promontory on the coast, which squeezed its inhabitants into a confined space, but it was not an island like Tyre (Herm 1975, 67). As will be discussed further below, Sidon was a timber center like Byblos and Tyre, but its importance ebbed when the other two cities were at weak points in their influence and power. While Byblos was the Phoenician city *par excellence* in the second millennium BC, Sidon was a close second and mentioned in numerous Amarna Letters. In fact, Sidon's position in the hierarchy of kingdoms in the ancient Near East was similar to Byblos' position, as one letter demonstrates: "Say to the king, my lord, my god, my Sun, the breath of my life: Thus Zimreddi, the mayor of Sidon. I fall at the feet of my lord, god, Sun, breath of my life, (at the feet of my lord, my god, my Sun, the breath of my life) 7 times and 7 times. May the king, my lord, know that Sidon, the maidservant of the king, my lord, which he put in my charge, is safe and sound." (Moran, 1992, 230)

Sidon may have been in an inferior position to Egypt during the middle to the late second millennium BC and less important than Tyre in the early first millennium BC, but by the 6th century BC, the geopolitical situation had drastically changed in the Near East and allowed Sidon to become politically important once more. When the Achaemenid Persian king Cambyses (530-522 BC) conquered Egypt in 525 BC, he and his people became the undisputed masters of the Near East, and during the Achaemenid period, which lasted until Alexander the Great conquered the region in 333 BC, Sidon was the regional headquarters of the empire (Markoe 2000, 51).

Under the Achaemenids, Sidon was one of the wealthiest cities in the empire, but it was also rebellious, and the 1st century BC Greek geographer and historian Strabo wrote about how the Sidonians used their wealth to rebel (albeit unsuccessfully) against Achaemenid king Artaxerxes III (359-338 BC): "Inasmuch as Sidon was distinguished for its wealth and its private citizens had amassed great riches from its shipping, many triremes were quickly outfitted and a multitude of mercenaries gathered, and, besides, arms, missiles, food, and all other materials useful in war were provided with dispatch" (Strabo, *Geography*, XVI, 41). Sidon would never again be an independent city, and the first millennium BC essentially marked the long decline of political independence in the Phoenician heartland.

The independence that the Phoenician cities enjoyed after the collapse of the Egyptian New Kingdom in the eighth century BC was short lived after the Assyrians stepped in to become the new imperial overlords of the Levant, as the Assyrian king Tiglath-Pileser III (747-727 BC) quickly subjugated the region (Markoe 2000, 41). The seafaring merchants of Phoenicia were no match for the Assyrian war machine, and they were quickly reduced to the status of tribute-paying vassals, similar to the situation they had with Egypt hundreds of years earlier. Assyrian historical annals relate the situation: "My official, the Rab-shaku, I sent to Tyre. From Metenna of Tyre I received 150 talents of gold . . . With the keen understanding and grasp of intellect with which the Master of the gods, the prince Nudimmut endowed me, a palace of cedar" (Luckenbill 1989, 1:288).

This source demonstrates that the Assyrians, like the Egyptians before them, coveted the timber of Phoenicia, but it also shows that the Phoenicians were subjected to harsh amounts of tribute. According to Assyrian records, the amount of 150 gold talents was actually the most they ever took as tribute from a conquered people (Markoe 2000, 50).

Chapter 3: Phoenician Culture

Writing and the Alphabet

Although the Assyrian conquest of Phoenicia marked the beginning of the end for the independence of Byblos, Tyre, and Sidon, the cities continued to produce an amazing and vibrant culture that influenced the world for centuries, and perhaps the most important, enduring, and well-known contribution the Phoenicians gave to the world was their form of writing, which would later influence subsequent forms both directly and indirectly.

There is no doubt that the alphabets and forms of writing employed by most European languages comes directly from the Phoenicians (Moscati 1968, 88), but the process that took place is still a mystery. Some of the ancient historians provide commentary and theories concerning how the Phoenicians gave their alphabet and system of writing to the Greeks, and Herodotus offered an account that is probably more accurate than most. It states: "The Phoenicians who came with Cadmus – amongst whom were the Gephyraei – introduced into

Greece, after their settlement in the country, a number of accomplishments, of which the most important was writing, an art till then, I think, unknown to the Greeks. At first they used the same characters as all the other Phoenicians, but as time went on, and they changed their language, they also changed the shape of their letters. At that period most of the Greeks in the neighborhood were Ionians; they were also taught these letters by the Phoenicians and adopted them, with a few alterations, for their own use, continuing to refer to them as Phoenician characters – as was only right, as the Phoenicians had introduced them" (Herodotus *Histories*, V, 58).

Like many of Herodotus' other passages in *Histories*, there is truth wrapped with some errors. The Greeks knew writing before the Phoenicians, as the Mycenaeans used the Linear B script, but that knowledge had vanished at the end of the Bronze Age (Morkot 1996, 18). Perhaps what makes Herodotus' account accurate and most interesting is his description of how the writing evolved. He mentions how the Greeks "changed the shape of their letters", which is the normal course when any group of people adopts a script to write their native language. For example, there are slight variations in the Latin script employed by most modern Western European languages, such as the umlauts in German or the various accents in French and Spanish. The Eastern European Cyrillic script is another example of how a group of people (the Slavs) took the Greek script and altered it to fit their own languages. Herodotus' account clearly demonstrates that the source he consulted was knowledgeable concerning the transfer of writing and scripts, and there is no reason to reject the assertion that it was the Phoenicians who first brought writing to Europe.

If the Phoenicians imparted their knowledge of writing to the Greeks, when, where, and how did the Phoenicians first learn how to write for themselves? As it turns out, writing, in various forms, was never a foreign concept to the ancient Phoenicians, no doubt due in part to the fact that the Phoenicians had close contact with many different peoples in the second millennium BC who knew writing, including as the Hittites, Babylonians, Egyptians, and other non-Phoenician peoples in the Levant. Scholars doubt that the cuneiform script of Mesopotamia influenced the Phoenicians, but the Egyptian hieroglyphic script, which had both phonetic and idiomatic elements, may have been an initial influence of the Phoenician alphabet (Moscati 1968, 89). Another possibility is that the Phoenician script originated with the Ugarit alphabet, in the non-Phoenician Levant city of Ugarit, around the 15th century BC (Moscati 1968, 89).

Whichever one of these was the ultimate inspiration for the Phoenician script may never be known, but it cannot be denied that the Phoenicians took that script and modified it to use simple, syllabic signs, which then spread to the Greeks and later to the Romans (Moscati 1968, 90-91).

Phoenician Religion

The Phoenician form of writing was the greatest contribution that culture made to the world, but it was their religion that set them apart from other peoples in the ancient Near East. The religion of the Phoenicians was similar in many ways to that of their neighbors in that it was polytheistic, and ritual played a large part in daily practice, but there were some unique aspects of it that played an important role in their culture.

Reconstructing the specifics of the Phoenician religion is difficult because the surviving extant Phoenician religious texts are brief and fragmentary (Moscati 1968, 30). Modern archeology may help provide some answers, but unfortunately, there is a dearth of religious structures, such as temples, that have survived until the present. That said, a temple discovered in the city of Kition on Cyprus is the largest Phoenician temple ever discovered and may provide an example of how similar temples in the Phoenician homeland (or even Solomon's Temple in Jerusalem) were constructed (Bikai 1989 207).

What modern scholars know of Phoenician religion seems to suggest that trade and religion were closely intertwined, as timber expeditions in the mountains of Lebanon also doubled as pilgrimages to Baalat, the goddess of Byblos (Herm 1975, 35). Like their neighbors, the Phoenician pantheon itself was amorphous, so each city had its own primary deity. For instance, Melqart was the primary god of Tyre, El/Baal was preeminent deity in Sidon, and the goddess Baalat – who had fertility attributes similar to the Mesopotamian Ishtar and the Egyptian Isis – stood supreme in Byblos (Moscati 1968, 31-34). Many of these deities possessed similar attributes, and one important aspect of myth that all the Phoenician cities shared was the importance of divine triads, meaning each city had a primary deity, his/her consort, and their offspring (Moscati 1968, 36).

As was often the case, characteristics of Phoenician deities likely assimilated traits from previous peoples' gods, and their own deities subsequently affected myths elsewhere. For example, the Old Testament's Book of Kings seems to make a mocking reference to Melqart that compares him to the Greeks' Hercules, while some Greek writers believed the Phoenicians worshiped their own Hercules. For example, Herodotus noted, "In the wish to get the best information that I could on these matters, I made a voyage to Tyre in Phoenicia, hearing there was a temple of Heracles at that place, very highly venerated. I visited the temple, and found it richly adorned with a number of offerings, among which were two pillars, one of pure gold, the other of smaragdos, shining with great brilliance at night. In a conversation which I held with the priests, I inquired how long their temple had been built, and found by their answer that they, too, differed from the Hellenes. They said that the temple was built at the same time that the city was founded, and that the foundation of the city took place 2,300 years ago. In Tyre I remarked another temple where the same god was worshipped as the Thasian Heracles. So I went on to Thasos, where I found a temple of Heracles which had been built by the Phoenicians who colonised that island when they sailed in search of Europa. Even this was five generations earlier than the time when Heracles, son of Amphitryon, was born in Hellas. These researches show plainly that there is an ancient god Heracles; and my own opinion is that those Hellenes act most wisely who build and maintain two temples of Heracles, in the one of which the Heracles worshipped is known by the name of Olympian, and has sacrifice offered to him as an immortal, while in the other the honours paid are such as are due to a hero."

The aspect of ancient Phoenician religion that set the Phoenicians farthest apart from their Near Eastern neighbors was the rituals they performed. Since they spent so much time on the seas trading and colonizing, water naturally played an important role in Phoenician religious rituals (Moscati 1968, 39). Like most of their neighbors, the Phoenicians also sacrificed animals to appease their gods, but unlike their neighbors, they also practiced human sacrifice during catastrophic times (Moscati 1968, 40). The practice of human sacrifice was carried with the Phoenicians to their many colonies, especially Carthage, where the Greeks wrote about the rituals with a combination of horror and amazement (which is discussed more thoroughly in the chapter about Carthage below).

A statue found in a Temple of Melqart on Cadiz

Phoenician Trade and Industry

If writing and the alphabet made the Phoenicians famous for posterity and their religion set them apart from their neighbors, then it was their industriousness and entrepreneurial spirit that made them a great civilization, because the wealth of Phoenicia was not built through imperialism but was a result of the commercial endeavors of the independent cities.

As noted before, the Phoenicians benefited from the emergence of the kingdom of Israel after the Israelites subjugated the Philistines, which allowed the Phoenicians to monopolize maritime trade in the Levant (Markoe 2000, 35). The Phoenicians not only developed sophisticated maritime trade routes, they also manufactured different products that were valued throughout the Mediterranean. Herodotus noted in book III of the *Histories* that the Phoenicians brought the gum storax into Greece, and they were also known for producing finished goods such as jewelry, carved ivory, bronze table vessels, bottled oils, and cloth dyed in "Tyrian purple" (Bikai 1989, 205). The substance known as Tyrian purple was a dye the Phoenicians extracted from the murex shellfish, which, when applied to white garments, turned them violet (Moscati 1968, 83). This purple dye is what the Greeks associated the Phoenicians with and may even be the origin of the name Phoenicia.

Although murex is the Phoenician commodity that most impressed the Greeks, it was their monopoly on the timber of the Levantine mountains that formed the basis of their wealth. Indeed, the most important factor in the economies of all the cities of the Phoenician heartland was timber, primarily cedar and fir, which they supplied to their timber-strapped neighbors (Moscati 1968, 83). There are a number of non-Phoenician primary texts that relate the importance of timber to the Phoenicians and their neighbors; a pseudo-historical Egyptian text known as the "Report of Wenamun," from the reign of Ramesses XI (ca. 1090-1080 BC) in the Twentieth Dynasty of the New Kingdom, relates the importance of the timber trade to both the Phoenicians and Egyptians. The story follows a royal official, Wenamun, as he leaves a politically fragmented and chaotic Egypt by boat, which is filled with Egyptian commodities and a priceless statue of the Egyptian god Amun. However, before Wenamun arrives in Byblos, he is robbed in the city of Dor by members of a former Sea People ethnic group known as the Tjeker, for which he retaliates by robbing another Tjeker ship before dropping anchor in Byblos. Wenamun's activities are apparently discovered by the king of Byblos, who is not happy: "They departed and I celebrated [in] a tent on the shore of the sea in the harbor of Byblos. And [I made a hiding place for] Amun-of-the-Road and place his possessions in it. Then the prince of Byblos sent to me saying: '[Leave my] harbor!' I sent to him, saying: 'Where shall [I go]?... If [you have a ship to carry me], let me be taken back to Egypt.' I spent twenty-nine days in his harbor, and he spent time sending to me daily to say: 'Leave my harbor!'" (Lichtheim 1976, 225).

This passage is most interesting because it demonstrates how the geopolitical tables were turned during this period. The king of Byblos is no longer a subservient minion who is forced to bow repeatedly before the mighty Egyptian pharaoh but is now in such a position of dominance that he can casually dismiss a royal Egyptian official.

As the story continues, Wenamun is finally able to convince the king of Byblos that he will be paid for the precious timber that the Egyptians need to build the sacred ship for the god Amun. The text reads, "The prince rejoiced. He assigned three hundred mean and three hundred oxen, and he set supervisors over them to have them fell the timbers. They were felled and they lay there during the winter. In the third month of summer they dragged them to the shore of the sea. The prince came out and stood by them, and he sent to me, saying: 'Come!' Now when I had been brought into his presence the shadow of his sunshade fell on me" (Lichtheim 1976, 228).

Byblos was clearly at the forefront of the Phoenician timber industry, but Tyre would also prove to be a major player in the trade and production of timber in the ancient Near East. As discussed above, King Hiram I of Tyre developed a close relationship with the kingdom of Israel, particularly during the reigns of kings David and Solomon, and in particular, Hiram and Phoenician timber are credited in the Old Testament for helping construct the Solomonic Temple. The Old Testament states: "And Solomon sent to Hiram saying. Thou knowest how that David my father could not build an house unto the name of the Lord his God for the wars which were about him on every side, until the Lord put them under the soles of his feet. But now the Lord my God hath given me rest on every side, so that there is neither adversary nor evil occurent. And, behold, I purpose to build an house unto the name of the Lord my God, as the Lord spake unto David my father, saying, 'Thy son, whom I will set upon thy throne in thy room, he shall build an house unto my name. Now therefore command thou that they hew me cedar trees out of Lebanon; and my servants shall be with thy servants: and unto thee will I give hire for thy servants according to all that thou shalt appoint: for thou knowest that there is not among us any that can skill to hew timber like unto the Sidonians. And it came to pass, when Hiram heard the words of Solomon, that he rejoiced greatly, and said, blessed by the Lord this day, which hath given unto David a wise son over this great people. And Hiram sent to Solomon, saying, 'I have considered the things which thou sentest to me for: and I will do all they desire concerning timber of cedar, and concerning timber of fir" (I Kings 5: 2-8). This passage relates that not only were the Phoenicians in possession of the coveted timber in the Levant, they were also expert lumberjacks, as "there is not among us any that can skill to hew timber like unto the Sidonians."

The Old Testament reveals that Solomon was extremely pleased with the final product of his temple and rewarded Hiram I handsomely for his efforts. Solomon, perhaps moved by what he viewed as desirable, decided to repay his ally Hiram I with a number of cities. The Old Testament states: "(Now Hiram the king of Tyre had furnished Solomon with cedar trees and fir trees, and with gold, according to all his desire,) that then king Solomon gave Hiram twenty cities in the land of Galilee. And Hiram came out from Tyre to see the cities which Solomon had given him; and they pleased him not. And he said, 'what cities are these which thou hast given me, my brother?' And he called them the land of Cabul unto this day" (I Kings 9:11-14). Hiram's reaction to being given control of numerous cities may seem at first a bit perplexing, but when readers consider this passage in its proper historical context, his actions seem more logical. Hiram I was the king of the Phoenician city of Tyre, and since the Phoenicians were not imperialists, what need would he have for more cities?

Clearly, the timber industry was crucial to the financial success of the Phoenician cities, and it became so much so that the Phoenicians expanded their logging activities beyond the mountains of the Levant. As the eighth century BC closed and the specter of the Assyrian Empire loomed on the horizon, the Phoenicians searched for new sources of timber beyond the forests of Lebanon (Watson-Treuman 2001, 75-76), and archaeological and textual evidence shows that the

Phoenicians exploited the Amanus mountain range (in what is today southeastern Turkey) for its cedar, juniper, and cypress trees (Watson-Treuman 2001, 77). This region was known as Cilicia in ancient times, and the Phoenician exploration, exploitation, and subsequent colonization of the region may have started in the 9th century BC (Watson-Treuman 2001, 82-82). The Phoenician timber colony in Cilicia was active for several hundred years, as the fourth century BC Greek historian Xenophon noted when he travelled through the region. He wrote, "From here a day's march through Syria of fifteen miles took Cyrus to Myriandrus, a city of on the sea, inhabited by Phoenicians. This place was a centre for trade and there many merchant ships at anchor there" (Xenophon, *The Persian Expedition*, I, 4, 3-5).

Although the Phoenicians moved some of their timber operations from the Phoenician heartland, Babylonian historical texts indicate that the Levant was still coveted for its trees in the 6th century BC. In fact, the famous Babylonian king Nebuchadnezzar II (604-562 BC) led a campaign into the Levant early in his reign with the intent of taking back trees to Babylon in order to beautify the temple of the god Marduk. One Babylonian text states, "(Trusting) in the power of my lords Nebo and Marduk, I organized [my army] for a[n expedition] to the Lebanon. I made that country happy by eradicating its enemy everywhere. All its scattered inhabitants I led back to their settlements. What no former kind had done (I achieved): I cut through steep mountains, I split rocks, opened passages and (thus) I constructed a straight road for the (transport of the) cedars. I made the Arahtu flo[at] (down) and carry to Marduk, my king, mighty cedars, high and strong, of precious beauty and of excellent dark quality, the abundant yield of the Lebanon, as (if they be) reed stalks (carried by) the river" (Pritchard 1992, 307).

Phoenician Exploration and Colonization

The Phoenician timber industry helped to make the cities of Byblos, Tyre, and Sidon wealthy, and this allowed the Phoenicians to partake in the activities that gained them the most respect from their contemporaries: exploration and colonization. An examination of Phoenician exploration and colonization reveals that although they were the most prolific travelers of the ancient world, their maritime technology was relatively equivalent to their neighbors. The Phoenicians used three basic type of ships: a war galley, a merchant ship, and a mussel boat that was a combination of the two (Herm 1975, 71).

If the Phoenicians' sailing prowess cannot be explained by any technological advantage they possessed over their contemporaries, then the answer must be that an intangible spirit and curiosity propelled them to unknown lands. The Greeks were particularly impressed with Phoenician exploration and wrote about the exploits of Phoenician mariners extensively. One particular achievement attributed to the Phoenicians was their sailing past and colonizing beyond the "Pillars of Hercules," which is what the ancient Greeks and Romans called the Straits of Gibraltar. Concerning these travels, Strabo wrote, "Again, the maritime supremacy of Minos is far-famed, and so are the voyages of the Phoenicians, who, a short time after the Trojan War, explored the regions beyond the Pillars of Hercules and founded cities both there and in the central parts of the Libyan sea-board" (Strabo, *Geography*, 1, 2). Modern scholars generally attribute the period of the Trojan Wars to around 1200 BC (Morkot 1996, 34), or around the period of the Sea Peoples invasions that would have placed the Phoenicians in the midst of the chaos, which they apparently avoided due to their superior maritime skills.

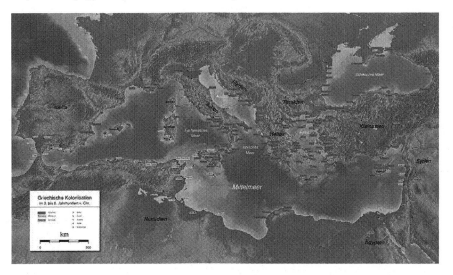

The yellow marks indicate Phoenician settlements across the Mediterranean in the 4th century BC. The red marks are Greek colonies.

Although sailing beyond the Straits of Gibraltar was truly an incredible feat for the time, the Phoenicians are also credited with a journey that still amazes people. According to Herodotus, the Egyptian king Nekau II (610-595 BC) commissioned a Phoenician expedition to sail around Libya – the word the Greeks used for all of Africa outside of Egypt. Apparently, the expedition began somewhere in the Nile Delta (probably the capital city of Memphis) and then travelled through man-made canals until it reached the Red Sea, where it began its long sea voyage. Herodotus wrote, "In view of what I have said, I cannot but be surprised at the method of mapping Libya, Asia, and Europe. The three continents do, in fact, differ very greatly in size. Europe is as long as the other two put together, and for breadth is not, in my opinion, even to be compared to them. As for Libya, we know that it is washed on all sides by the sea except where it joins Asia, as was first demonstrated, so far as our knowledge goes, by the Egyptian king Neco, who, after calling off the construction of the canal between the Nile and the Arabian gulf, sent out a fleet manned by a Phoenician crew with orders to sail round and return to Egypt and the Mediterranean by way of the Pillars of Heracles. The Phoenicians sailed from the Red Sea into the southern ocean, and every autumn put in where they were on the Libyan coast, sowed a patch of ground, and waited for next year's harvest. Then, having got in their grain, they put to sea again, and after two full years rounded the Pillars of Heracles in the course of the third, and returned to Egypt. These men made a statement which I do not myself believe, though others may, to the effect that as they sailed on a westerly course round the southern end of Libya, they had the sun on their right – to northward of them. This is how Libya was first discovered to be surrounded by sea, and the next people to make a similar report were the Carthaginians" (Herodotus, *Histories*, IV, 42-43).

This passage reveals some interesting points, particularly the fact that Herodotus does not believe the account without stating his reasons. Perhaps he found the crew's statement of the position of the sun confusing and unbelievable and therefore deduced that they lied, but the science supports the account. If they sailed around Africa starting in the Indian Ocean, then the sun would have been exactly where Herodotus stated it was. At this point, Herodotus' account cannot be corroborated by any other primary sources, but it is amazing to consider that a crew of Phoenicians may have been the first people to circumnavigate Africa, which they would have accomplished over 2,000 before Vasco de Gama did it for Portugal in the late 15th century.

Phoenician Military Endeavors

The Phoenicians were clearly the masters of the Mediterranean Sea in the ancient world, which placed them in demand for more than just trade and exploration. Although the Phoenicians are not known today for their martial abilities, their prowess as mariners was utilized by different ancient peoples, especially the Persians, in naval actions.

The first major historical accounts of the Phoenicians being involved in naval battles was related by Herodotus and pertained to the Persian Wars (499-479 BC) fought by Greece and the Persian Empire. As noted earlier, Phoenicia became part of the Achaemenid Empire when Cambyses conquered the rich territory in the late 6th century BC, but unlike the Egyptians, Assyrians, and Babylonians before him, the Persian king valued the Phoenician sailors more than the region's timber. Since the Achaemenid Persians' homeland was essentially a mountainous region, they had no navy with which to invade Europe, and the Phoenicians helped solve the Persians' maritime quandary by being conscripted into the Achaemenid army and used for their naval skills.

It seems the Phoenician sailors acquitted themselves well in battle, especially during the initial Persian invasion of Europe around the Black Sea. Herodotus wrote, "The people of Byzantium, and their opposite neighbors in Chalcedon, instead of awaiting the attack of the Phoenicians by sea, abandoned their homes and fled to the Black Sea coast, where they established themselves at Mesembria. The Phoenicians, after destroying by fire the places I have mentioned, turned their attention to Proconnesus and Artace; then, having burnt these too, they returned to the hersonese to take such places as had escaped destruction on their previous visit. The one exception was

Cyzicus; for before the Phoenicians entered the strait, the people of this town had made their submission to Darius by coming to terms with Oebares, the son of Magabazus, who was governor of Dascyleium. Thus all the towns of the Chersonese, except Cardia, were taken by the Phoenicians" (Herodotus, *Histories,* VI, 33).

The Phoenicians continued to fight with the Persian army, led later by King Xerxes (486-465 BC), and they contributed 300 ships to the pivotal Battle of Salamis in 480 BC (Herodotus, *Histories*, VII, 89). The Battle of Salamis proved to be the turning point not only in the Persian Wars (as the defeated Persians never tried to conquer Europe again) but also for the military power of the Phoenicians, which was greatly diminished from that period forward. For his part, Herodotus relates that the Phoenicians were probably unduly blamed for the Persian loss: "The greatest destruction took place when the ships which had been first engaged turned tail; for those stationed behind fell foul of them in their attempt to press forward and do some service before the eyes of the king. In the confusion which resulted, some Phoenicians who had lost their ships came to Xerxes and tried to make out that the loss was due to the treachery of the Ionians. But the upshot was that it was they themselves, and not the Ionian captains, who were executed for misbehaviour. While they were speaking, a ship of Samothrace rammed an Athenian; the Athenian was going down, when an Aeginetan vessel bore down upon the Somothracian and sank her, but the Samothracian crew, who were armed with javelins, cleared the deck of the attacking vessel, lept aboard, and captured her. This exploit saved the Ionians; for when Xerxes saw an Ionian ship do such a fine piece of work, he turned to the Phoenicians and, ready as he was in his extreme vexation to find fault with anyone, ordered their heads to be cut off, to stop them from casting cowardly aspersions upon their betters" (Herodotus, *Histories*, VIII, 89-90).

Despite their losses and treatment at the hands of Xerxes, the Phoenicians continued to be a part of the Achaemenid Empire after the Persian Wars, so they were required to take part in more wars. In fact, the Phoenicians provided the bulk of the navy for the Persians until the late 4th century BC, when Alexander the Great swept through the Near East and toppled kingdom after kingdom. However, the 2nd century AD Roman historian Arrian recounts that despite the diminished status of the Phoenician navy, it still commanded respect from Alexander and the Greeks. He wrote, "Alexander replied that Parmenio was mistaken, and that he had wrongly interpreted the omen. In the first place, it was absurd to rush blindly into a naval engagement against greatly superior forces, and with an untrained fleet against the highly trained Cyprian and Phoenician crews; the sea, moreover, was a tricky thing – one could not trust it, and he was not going to risk making a present to the Persians of all the skill and courage of his men" (Arrian, *The Campaigns of Alexander*, I, 18).

Andrew Dunn's picture of an ancient bust of Alexander the Great

Chapter 4: Carthage

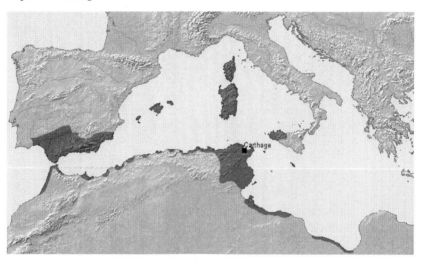

The Carthaginian Empire in the 3rd century B.C. before the Punic Wars.

Ultimately, Alexander the Great's conquests left Phoenician naval power and cities decimated, but thanks to their colonization, Phoenician influence could still be found around the Mediterranean, especially in the form of an empire that rivaled the power of the Greeks and Romans. The ancient city of Carthage, which was located in modern Tunisia, would ultimately grow from a small Phoenician colony into one of the great powers of the Mediterranean.

Carthage is one of the best known cities of antiquity, but a peculiarity of Carthaginian historiography is that, either due to its destruction at the hands of the Romans or because it simply did not have a particularly strong written tradition, very few written materials from the city survive. Although some inscriptions still exist and scholars understand their language, the overwhelming majority of sources for the period are Greek and Roman. This presents readers with a problem, because Greece and Rome were both in conflict with Carthage at one time or another for centuries. The result is a highly biased historiography which does not cast Carthage in a particularly positive light and may simply be wrong altogether, something which is worth taking into account when reviewing the history of the city as it's understood today. A further issue which has frequently befuddled historians is that, from the advent of the Magonid dynasty onwards, virtually all important figures in Carthage were named Mago, Hannibal, Hamilcar, Hasdrubal, Hanno, or Gisco, and they have found little help from sources or materials that can help them distinguish one from the other.

Though the ancient historians, basing their accounts on mythological theories, argued that

Carthage was founded around 1250 B.C., modern archaeological exploration suggests that a figure of circa 850 BC is more correct. Perhaps the most famous ancient myth in circulation was that Queen Elissar, better known as Queen Dido, founded Carthage. This found currency among both Greek and Roman sources. In his famous text *Geography*, Strabo wrote:

> "Carthage is situated upon a peninsula, comprising a circuit of 360 stadia, with a wall, of which sixty stadia in length are upon the neck of the peninsula, and reach from sea to sea. Here the Carthaginians kept their elephants, it being a wide open place. In the middle of the city was the acropolis, which they called Byrsa, a hill of tolerable height with dwellings round it. On the summit was the temple of Esculapius, which was destroyed when the wife of Asdrubas burnt herself to death there, on the capture of the city. Below the Acropolis were the harbors and the Cothon, a circular island, surrounded by a canal communicating with the sea (Euripus), and on every side of it (upon the canal) were situated sheds for vessels.

> Carthage was founded by Dido, who brought her people from Tyre. Both this colony and the settlements in Spain and beyond the Pillars proved so successful to the Phoenicians, that even to the present day they occupy the best parts on the continent of Europe and the neighboring islands. They obtained possession of the whole of Africa, with the exception of such parts as could only be held by nomad tribes. From the power they acquired they raised a city to rival Rome…"

Despite the stories about the famous Queen Dido, and the fact that the sprawling Carthage likely did not control 300 other settlements, Carthage was almost certainly founded during the colonization boom of the Phoenician Empire. This was a movement which took advantage of the relative collapse in the fortunes of Greece, Crete and the Hittite Empire to establish a string of up to 3,000 colonies between Asia Minor and Spain, and Carthage was conveniently positioned smack in the middle of the extremely lucrative Iberia–Asia Minor raw metals route. Although it was a convenient position, Carthage itself was apparently not intended to be anything special in terms of colonizing efforts, particularly because the Phoenician colonial method differed radically from the Greek variant. While the Hellenes would create a settlement that was self-sustaining and almost always self-governing, while still retaining ties of alliance and friendship with the so-called "Mother City" on mainland Greece, the Phoenicians, both for administrative control reasons and due to population constraints, did not as a rule create self-sufficient colonies. Instead, the Phoenicians exerted more control over the settlements, particularly when it came to trade regulations. Thus, the settlement which gradually spread upon the hill of Byrsa was very low in the food chain. Initially, Carthage paid tribute to the local Lybian tribes to avoid being attacked and had a governor (sometimes incorrectly labeled "King" by ancient Greek sources) who had most likely been imposed upon them from Tyre. Carthage, however, was fortunate in having a larger neighbor, the Phoenician city of Utica, which provided them with significant economic and trade assistance during the colony's early years. That was a decision Utica would later regret when Carthage grew in size and eclipsed it entirely.

From 850–650 BC, Carthage gradually became wealthier thanks to the city's privileged position straddling the major land and sea trade routes of the Mediterranean. These two centuries saw the emergence of what would later become known as "Punic" (Carthaginian) culture, a distinctly West African Phoenician identity which differed noticeably from its predecessor. The growth of this culture indicated a rise in influence on Carthage's part, and that rise manifested itself in 650 BC when Carthage founded its own independent colony, a settlement on Ibiza, without assistance from Tyre. As the fortunes of Tyre and the Phoenician Empire waned, first with the loss of Sicily to the ever-expanding Greeks and then with Nebuchadnezzar of Babylon's great siege of Tyre in 585 B.C., Carthage's fortunes continued to rise. More settlements were founded, more cities of the North African seaboard were brought under direct Carthaginian control rather than paying their dues to Tyre, and a large colony was established in Syrtis, between Tunisia and Lybia. Additionally, Carthage's rise was bolstered by the influx of a large number of immigrants of both wealth and high political status from Tyre itself, as many of the elite fled the conflicts which enveloped the Phoenician capital.

Even as Carthage's influence began to grow and neighboring settlements like Utica began to suffer, the Carthaginians managed to remain on good terms with most of their neighbors. Although wars are said to have taken place against the Mauri, Numidians and Libyans at various points between 850-650 B.C., there seems to have been a genuine reluctance, for reasons of policy, by the Carthaginians to expand their territorial domains on the African mainland. This includes the very environs of Carthage itself, for which the Carthaginians paid a tributary lease to the Libyans until at least 550 B.C. Similarly, despite their *de facto* independence, Carthage continued to send Tyre an annual tribute destined for their founder-god for centuries. Despite these tributes, however, there was no doubt that a new power had leapt upon the Mediterranean scene. The Carthaginian hegemony was emerging.

The Phoenicians of Carthage retained many aspects of Phoenician culture, most notably their merchant and exploration activities, and most of the Phoenician colonies in the western Mediterranean Sea that Strabo mentioned in the above passage, which included coastal Spain, became Carthaginian possessions by the middle of the 4th century BC (Moscati 1968, 234). It was from those ports that the Carthaginians were able to apply their seaman skills, and Herodotus wrote about the Carthaginians trading with a group of people in Libya from "beyond the Pillars of Hercules": "The Carthaginians also say that they trade with a race of men who live in a part of Libya beyond the Pillars of Heracles. On reaching this country, they unload their goods, arrange them tidily along the beach, and then, returning to their boats, raise a smoke. Seeing the smoke, the natives come down to the beach, place on the ground a certain quantity of gold in exchange for the goods, and go off again to a distance. The Carthaginians then come ashore and take a look at the gold; and if they think it represents a fair price for their wares, they collect it and go away; if, on the other, it seems too little, they go aboard and wait, and the natives come and add to the gold until they are satisfied. There is perfect honesty on both sides; the Carthaginians never touch the gold until it equals in value what they have offered for sale, and the natives never touch the goods until the gold has been taken away" (Herodotus, *Histories*, IV, 196).

The land Herodotus wrote about could possibly be somewhere in sub-Saharan Africa, but without corroborating texts or archaeological evidence, it is difficult to say for sure. As Carthage grew more powerful, its people and the people of the Phoenician heartland maintained ties and recognized their kinship. The Persian king Cambyses even desired to conquer Carthage after his successful campaign in Egypt, but he was stymied by his Phoenician-led navy, who refused to fight against their kinsmen. Herodotus noted, "The Phoenicians, however, refused to go, because of the close bond which connected Phoenicia and Carthage, and the wickedness of making war against their own children. In this way, with the Phoenicians out of it and the remainder of the naval force too weak to undertake the campaign alone, the Carthaginians escaped Persian domination" (Herodotus, *Histories,* III, 19). This passage is important, because it not only depicts the close ties between Carthage and the other Phoenicians but also demonstrates that the Phoenicians changed the course of history by not going to war against Carthage. When the Phoenicians refused to invade Carthage, Cambyses was forced to change his plans, which ultimately led to his successor, Darius I, invading Greece.

Although the Phoenicians maintained close ties with the Carthaginians, the culture of Carthage developed independently and eventually became a unique culture that was in some ways very different than the Phoenician homeland. The early settlers of Carthage spoke the Phoenician language identical to that spoken in Tyre, but by the 6th century BC, it had evolved into a distinct dialect that became known as "Punic" (Markoe 2000, 114). The use of Punic spread throughout the western Mediterranean region, and a new script also developed along with the spoken dialect (Markoe 2000, 114). The spoken language of Punic borrowed some aspects of Greek and Latin grammar, but historians contend that differences between Phoenician and Punic were minor and only go to prove the continuity of Phoenician culture in Carthage (Moscati 1968, 186).

As the Phoenician language evolved when it spread to Carthage, the religion also made similar transitions. Initially, the Carthaginian pantheon reflected that of the Phoenician homeland, but over time it evolved and was influenced by Libyan, Numidian, Greek, and Roman elements (Moscati 1968, 137). Tanit and Baal Hammon were the most important Carthaginian deities, but Melqart of Tyre was also important since he was the patron of the city where Carthage's inhabitants originated (Moscati 1968, 139). For the most part, the ritual aspects of Carthaginian religion were similar to those practiced in Phoenicia, but sacrifices, especially human sacrifices, were much more important in Carthage (Moscati 1968, 141). The Carthaginians, like their

Phoenician ancestors, reserved human sacrifice for especially desperate times, and children were often the victims. The 1st century BC Greek historian Diodorus relates how the Carthaginians sacrificed hundreds of their own children after a devastating defeat by Agathocles and his Greek army in 310 BC: "They also alleged that Cronus had turned against them inasmuch as in former times they had been accustomed to sacrifice to this god the noblest of their sons, but more recently, secretly buying and nurturing children, they had sent these to the sacrifice; and when an investigation was made, some of those who had been sacrificed were discovered to have been substitutions. When they had given thought to these things and saw their enemy encamped before their walls, they were filled with superstitious dread, for they believed that they had neglected the honours of the gods that had been established by their fathers. In their zeal to make amends for their omission, they selected two hundred of the noblest children and sacrificed them publicly; and others who were under suspicion sacrificed themselves voluntarily, in number not less than three hundred. There was in their city a bronze image of Cronus, extending its hands, palms up and sloping toward the ground, so that each of the children when placed thereon rolled down and fell into a sort of gaping pit filled with fire" (Diodorus, *The Library of History*, XX, 14, 4-6).

Human sacrifice is considered barbaric and illogical today, but the Carthaginians believed that by sacrificing their own children, the gods would view them in a propitious manner. As the war waged on between Agathocles and the Carthaginians, the tide turned, and in 307 BC the Carthaginians won a major battle, which resulted in more human sacrifices, but this time they sacrificed Greek prisoners as a token of thanks to the Carthaginian pantheon. Diodorus wrote, "While the Carthaginians after their victory were sacrificing the fairest of their captives as thank-offerings to the gods by night, and while a great blaze enveloped the men who were being offered as victims, a sudden blast of wind struck them, with the result that the sacred hut, which was near the altar, caught fire" (Diodorus, *The Library of History*, XX, 65, 1).

Human sacrifice, especially of children, was an aspect of Carthaginian religion that clearly set them apart from their neighbors, but the Carthaginians also adapted to their surroundings by adopting some of their non-Phoenician neighbors' cultural ideas. As Carthage formed its own culture, it established its own unique social structure, which borrowed some aspects of Phoenician, African, and even Greek society and melded it into their own. Foremost among the social orders were Carthaginian citizens, who remained an exclusive and tight-knit body with none of the inclusive policies adopted by the Romans or some Greek *poleis*, which allowed aliens to eventually assume citizenship in return for certain services. Carthaginian citizens were usually involved in either politics or trade, which was made all the more lucrative because this select group was exempt from taxation. At the same time, since most citizens were involved in commerce, Carthage grew to rely heavily on mercenary and auxiliary armies, since having a citizen army in the field would cripple the city economically. Those citizens not involved in trading were frequently in political office in one of Carthage's colonies, as Carthage insisted on exerting direct political control over the settlements they established.

Though not citizens, a similar preferential status was enjoyed by the tributary allies that Carthage obtained as her influence grew. These cities were allowed a relatively high degree of self-governance, though they were forced to cede all trading control and foreign relations to Carthage and provide contingents for a joint Punic Army and Navy, which in turn helped police the Carthaginian economic empire. Furthermore, operating as something of a racketeering policy, the Carthaginian military offered protection to allies against bandits and pirates.

The lowest end of the social scale was occupied by the conquered people in the area directly surrounding Carthage. Following successive pushes into the interior from 650-580 BC, Carthage subdued a number of Lybian cities, whose inhabitants were required to raze their walls, surrender their entire administration to Carthaginian officials, serve in the Punic Army as the lowest of arrow fodder, and pay an exorbitant tribute that could be as high as half their region's agricultural output.

The government of Carthage may have been even more profoundly influenced by Roman culture. Carthage was ruled over by a king in its early history (Moscati 1968, 131), which later gave way to a multi-cameral government that included a Senate composed of about 300 members (Moscati 1968, 132). The Roman historian Livy wrote about how the Carthaginian Senate conducted its affairs before and during the Second Punic War (218-202 BC), and according to him, the famed Carthaginian general Hannibal had to acquire the acceptance of the Senate before he could even join the military: "Years before, when Hannibal was little more than a boy, Hasdrubal had written home to request his presence with the troops, and the propriety of the request had been debated in the Carthaginian Senate. The Barca party was in favour of granting it, urging the wisdom of accustoming the young man to active service, with a view to his ultimate succession of his father's position, but the opposite view was taken by their opponents" (Livy, *War with Hannibal*, XXI, 3).

Based on Livy's description, the Carthaginian government resembled the Roman Republic more than a Near Eastern despotic monarchy. Not only did the Carthaginians have to go through their Senate before undertaking any serious endeavors, but the Senate was rife with feuding factions, which was another similarity to the Roman government.

The Carthaginian government was fundamentally different from those in the Phoenician homeland, but perhaps the most important difference between the Carthaginians and their Phoenician ancestors was the Carthaginian military prowess. The Carthaginians were Phoenician in most aspects of their culture, but they differed from their cousins in their ability and willingness to use military force to acquire new territories. The Carthaginians were involved in wars with the Greeks, which eventually resulted in Carthaginian control of Sicily (Crawford 2001, 34), but it was war with the Romans that ultimately established their reputation as warriors, even if it also brought forth the decline of their society. Over a period of slightly more than 100 years, the Carthaginians and Romans fought three wars against each other that determined the course of history in the Mediterranean region and left the Carthaginians vanquished.

Matters looked grim for Carthage during the First Punic War when Rome, after a string of victorious naval and land battles, took the fight to North Africa, advancing into the Carthaginian heartland. Only a last-ditch defense by the mercenary general Xanthippus at the Battle of Tunis in 241, when the Roman cavalry found itself utterly outnumbered and the Roman legions were forced to face the shock of Punic war elephants, saved Carthage from a siege. Having suffered a grievous reversal, the Romans decided it was time to seek peace, but they did so from a position of utter supremacy. For the first time since they had first gotten involved in Sicilian affairs, Carthage was forced to surrender the entire island to Roman control, as well as pay a colossal war indemnity. Additionally, Rome also secured the release of 8,000 prisoners of war without paying a penny in ransom, blows which badly crippled the Carthaginian economy.

The result of the First Punic War was a complete dearth of cash in Carthage, which was a serious problem because Carthage relied chiefly on mercenary armies. Thousands of mercenaries throughout the Carthaginian Empire were suddenly not getting their wages, and the result was inevitable: war. An all-out insurrection of mercenary contingents throughout the Punic Empire, including Iberia, Sardinia and Corsica, and a renewed attack from the subjugated Lybian tribes, followed. Suddenly, Carthage was fighting for her very life, and grudgingly accepting military and financial aid from her two old enemies, Syracuse and Rome.

The war dragged on for two years, but by 238 Carthage was once again secure, with order restored to her dominions. Still, the cost had been heavy; taking advantage of Carthage's desperate situation, Rome had conveniently seized both Sardinia and Corsica, which had been plunged into lawlessness by the mercenary uprising, and there was nothing Carthage could do about it. The mines of Iberia, with their vast amounts of as yet untapped wealth, were still secure, but control of them was dubious.

Crisis, as so often occurs, had brought political change in its wake, and the Barcid family, led by Hamilcar Barca, had risen to prominence during the Mercenary Wars. Hamilcar was a skilled general who rapidly rose to command all of the Carthaginian armies by ousting the competition of his rival, Hanno the Great. Hamilcar was populist and had the support of the common people, whereas Hanno was a scion of the old Carthaginian aristocracy, but their power was on the wane. Thus, it was Hamilcar and his son-in-law, Hasdrubal the Fair, who subdued the Iberian cities, but the loyalty of these new dominions was far from certain. Rather than owing allegiance to Carthage, the Iberian cities looked to Hamilcar exclusively for guidance, making Spain a virtual Barcid fief.

It was during the Second Punic War that the Carthaginians demonstrated their martial abilities and nearly defeated Rome. The Carthaginians were led by Hannibal Barca, who introduced new tactics that confused and defeated the Romans in several crushing battles, but he is best known for leading a large army from Spain across the Alps and into Italy, where he stayed for nearly 16 years while pillaging and looting the countryside of the south. Hannibal's passage of the Alps remains the most famous event of his life and legend, and even though the location of his crossing matters little compared to the fact that he ultimately did get across, it has nonetheless been the most compelling mystery of his life for over 2,000 years. Even ancient historians were intrigued and tried to figure out the answer. The well known ancient Greek historian Polybius mentioned that Hannibal's men came into conflict with a Celtic tribe, the Allobroges, which was situated near the northern part of the range along the banks of the river Isère. The famous Roman historian Livy, writing over 150 years after Polybius, claimed Hannibal took a southerly route.

It is believed that both historians used the same source, a soldier in Hannibal's army, Sosylus of Lacedaemon, who wrote a history of the Second Punic War. Geographers and historians have pointed to the 6 most likely mountain passes that could have actually been used and then tried to narrow it down by finding one that seems to match the descriptions of both Livy and Polybius. A handful of historians used those accounts to theorize that Hannibal crossed the Alps at the **Col** du Montgenèvre pass, which would have been in the southern part of the range near northwest Italy. That also happened to be one of the better known road passes in the ancient world, and it was used often for diplomacy.

Hannibal. (Noapel, National-Museum.)

Bust of Hannibal

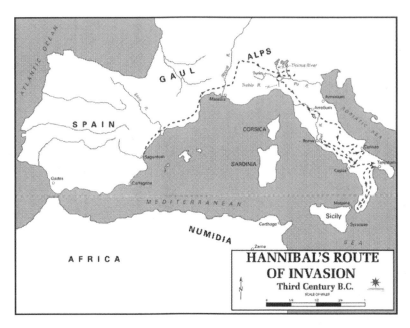

Estimated March of Hannibal's Invasion of Italy by the United States Military Academy

Furthermore, Hannibal's annihilation of a Roman army at Cannae is still considered one of the greatest tactical victories in the history of warfare. Hannibal's troops in the center yielded before the legions, as Hannibal had anticipated, sucking the bulk of the Roman force deep into the centre of Hannibal's formation. Meanwhile, the wings of Hannibal's infantry automatically swung against the flanks of the Roman force while Hannibal's cavalry, led by his celebrated general Maharbal, crushed the Roman cavalry and light infantry deployed to protect the formation's flanks and rear and, in so doing, succeeded in encircling it completely. The Roman force now found itself unable to run or maneuver, completely surrounded by Hannibal's forces. It was one of the earliest examples of the pincer movement in the history of warfare. As military historian Theodore Dodge described, "Few battles of ancient times are more marked by ability...than the battle of Cannae. The position was such as to place every advantage on Hannibal's side. The manner in which the far from perfect Hispanic and Gallic foot was advanced in a wedge in échelon... was first held there and then withdrawn step by step, until it had reached the converse position... is a simple masterpiece of battle tactics. The advance at the proper moment of the African infantry, and its wheel right and left upon the flanks of the disordered and crowded Roman legionaries, is far beyond praise. The whole battle, from the Carthaginian standpoint, is a consummate piece of art, having no superior, few equal, examples in the history of war."

Ultimately, however, Hannibal had to return to North Africa to protect Carthage, and it was near the city that he was finally defeated by the Roman general Scipio at the Battle of Zama in 202 BC (Scarre 1996, 24). Although the Carthaginians lost the Second Punic War, they remained enough of a power in the region to continue to challenge Roman authority, which was met with the full might of the Roman military during the Third Punic War (Bagnall 2002, 68).

With no mercenaries to rely upon for military clout, the Carthaginians were forced to turn virtually the entire city population into a militia, manning the walls and stubbornly resisting Roman attempts to seize Carthage for as long as three years. Finally, in 146, the troops of Scipio Aemilianus breached the walls and stormed the city. What followed was a complete annihilation. The Romans first fired every Carthaginian vessel docked in the harbor before moving systematically through the city, tearing down houses one by one, slaughtering their inhabitants and keeping only those deemed useful as slaves. When they were done reducing the city to rubble, popular legend has it that the legionaries sowed salt onto its ashes to ensure nothing would ever grow there again.

With Carthage destroyed, the Romans had effectively ended Phoenician influence in the western Mediterranean region, and Carthage became part of the Roman province of Africa (Bagnall 2002, 75).

Chapter 5: The Decline of the Phoenician Homeland

The dramatic end of Phoenician culture in Carthage was actually a mirror of what happened nearly 200 years before in Phoenicia. As Alexander the Great and the Macedonians rose to power in the late 4th century BC and eventually conquered the Achaemenid Empire, the Persians were not their only victims. Since the Phoenicians had supported the Persians for so long, they decided to hold out against Alexander and his army, which proved to be a fatal decision.

Alexander's attempts at pacifying the region in short order were greatly frustrated by Tyre, which had colossal fortifications that required the construction of siege works and engines of war on a massive scale to reduce, and the resistance from Tyre's garrison was exceedingly fierce. As a result, when Alexander did take Tyre, the citizens suffered his wrath. The Greek historian Diodorus wrote:

> "Alexander addressed the Macedonians, calling on them to dare no less than he. Fitting out all his ships for fighting, he began a general assault upon the walls by land and sea and this was pressed furiously. He saw that the wall on the side of the naval base was weaker than elsewhere, and brought up to that point his triremes lashed together and supporting his best siege engines. Now he performed a feat of daring which was hardly believable even to those who saw it. He flung a bridge across from the wooden tower to the city walls and crossing by it alone gained a footing on the wall, neither concerned for the envy of Fortune nor fearing the

menace of the Tyrians. Having as witness of his prowess the great army which had defeated the Persians, he ordered the Macedonians to follow him, and leading the way he slew some of those who came within reach with his spear, and others by a blow of his sabre. He knocked down sill others with the rim of his shield, and put an end to thigh confidence of the enemy.

Simultaneously in another part of the city the battering ram, put to its work, brought down a considerable stretch of the wall; and when the Macedonians entered through this breach and Alexander's party poured over the bridge on to the wall, the city was taken. The Tyrians, however, kept up the resistance with mutual cries of encouragement and blocked the alleys with barricades, so that all except a few were cut down fighting, in number more than seven thousand. The king sold the women and children into slavery and crucified all the men of military age" (Diodorus, *The Library of* History, XVII, 46).

Although the surviving Phoenicians were pacified after Alexander's destruction of Tyre, and some even joined him against the Persians, the Phoenician culture was effectively destroyed. Modern archaeological evidence also shows that after Alexander's campaign, the number of Phoenician goods in the region dissipated, even from the areas where the Phoenicians were the most numerous (Berlin 1997, 75). By examining pottery remains, archaeologists have determined that in the period immediately after Alexander's conquest of the Levant, "a specific Phoenician cultural identity had evaporated, to the point where their physical presence is no longer distinguishable in that region's archaeological record" (Berlin 1996, 88). Ironically, this may have been due to the Phoenicians' ability and willingness to assimilate other cultures' art patterns and styles, making it virtually impossible to distinguish Phoenician remains from others' remains.

In the end, and despite the fact they had profoundly influenced both civilizations, the Phoenicians were unable to withstand the military might of the Greeks and Romans.

Bibliography

Arrian. 1971. *The Campaigns of Alexander.* Translated by Aubrey de Sélincourt. London: Penguin Books.

Bagnall, Nigel. 2002. *The Punic Wars: 246-146 BC.* London: Osprey Publishing.

Berlin, Andrea M. 1997. "From Monarchy to Markets: The Phoenicians in Hellenistic Palestine." *Bulletin of the American Schools of Oriental Research* 306: 75-88.

Bikai, Patricia Maynor. 1989. "Cyprus and the Phoenicians." *Biblical Archaeologist* 52: 203 209.

Breasted, James Henry, ed. and trans. 2001. *Ancient Records of Egypt*. Vol. 2, *The Eighteenth Dynasty*. Chicago: University of Illinois Press.

Cochavi-Rainey, Zipora, trans and ed. 1999. *Royal Gifts in the Late Bronze Age Fourteenth to Thirteenth Centuries B.C.E.: Selected Texts Recording Gifts to Royal Personages*. Jerusalem: Ben-Gurion University of the Negev Press.

Crawford, Michael. 2001. "Early Rome and Italy." In *The Oxford history of the Roman world*, ed. John Boardman, Jasper Griffin, and Oswyn Murray, 50-73. Oxford: Oxford University Press.

Diodorus. 2004. *The Library of History*. Translated by C.H. Oldfather. Cambridge, Massachusetts: Harvard University Press.

Herm, Gerhard. 1975. *The Phoenicians: The Purple Empire of the Ancient Near East*. Translated   by Caroline Hillier. New York: William Morrow and Company.

Herodotus. 2003. *The Histories*. Translated by Aubrey de Sélincourt. London: Penguin Books.

Kuhrt, Amélie. 2010. *The Ancient Near East: c. 3000-330 BC*. 2 vols. London: Routledge.

Lichtheim, Miriam, ed. 1976. *Ancient Egyptian Literature*. Vol. 2, *The New Kingdom*. Los Angeles: University of California Press.

Livy. 1996. *The War with Hannibal*. Translated by Aubrey de Sélincourt. London: Penguin Books.

Lloyd, Alan B. 1975. "Were Necho's Triremes Phoenician?" *Journal of Hellenic Studies* 95: 45-   61.

Lucas, A. and J.R. Harris. 1999. *Ancient Egyptian Materials and Industries*. Mineola, New York: Dover Publications.

Luckenbill, Daniel David, trans. and ed. 1989. *Ancient Records of Assyria and Babylonia*. 2 vols.   London: Histories and Mysteries of Man.

Markoe, Glenn E. 2000. *Phoenicians*. Los Angeles: University of California Press.

Moran, William L. ed. and trans. 1992. *The Amarna Letters*. Baltimore: John Hopkins University   Press.

Morkot, Robert. 1996. *The Penguin Historical Atlas of Ancient Greece*. London: Penguin Books.

Moscati, Sabatino. 1968. *The World of the Phoenicians*. Translated by Alastair Hamilton. New York: Frederick A. Praeger.

Noureddine, Ibrahim. 2010. "New Light on the Phoenician Harbor at Tyre." *Near Eastern Archaeology* 73: 176-181.

Pritchard, James B, ed. 1992. *Ancient Near Eastern Texts Relating to the Old Testament*. 3rd ed. Princeton, New Jersey: Princeton University Press.

Scarre, Chris. 1995. *The Penguin Historical Atlas of Ancient Rome*. London: Penguin Books.

Stern, E. 1990. "New Evidence from Dor for the First Appearance of the Phoenicians along the Northern Coast of Israel." *Bulletin of the American Schools of Oriental Research* 279: 27-34.

Strabo. 2001. *Geography*. Translated by Horace Leonard Jones. Cambridge, Massachusetts: Harvard University Press.

Watson-Treumann, Brigette. 2001. "Beyond the Cedars of Lebanon: Phoenician Timber Merchants and Trees from the 'Black Mountain.'" *Die Welt des Orients* 31: 75-83.

Wright, Edmund, ed. 2006. *A Dictionary of World History*. 2nd ed. Oxford: Oxford University Press.

Xenophon. 1972. *The Persian Expedition*. Translated by Rex Warner. London: Penguin Books.

Made in the USA
Middletown, DE
05 September 2018